Change Your Own Economy

People I wish to thank for positively impacting my life.

Brother Peter, our exceptional mind motivating sports coach, Patrician College Dublin.
Eamon Daly, business/commerce teacher, communicator, Patrician College Dublin.
Pat Timmons my team manager and mentor at Erin's Isle GAA Club.
Pat Bobbett, the heart and soul of Ashbourne Rugby Club.

Nina, wife and partner who always believed in me and never gave up, regardless of my wild and stubborn ways.
To My children who have blessed my life and from whom I will continue to learn.

Edited By James Van De Waal

This book is dedicated to the memory of Napoleon Hill.

Change Your Own Economy

Chapter 1

Let There Be Light

If you have attracted this book into your life then you are probably ready for it.

Firstly let me congratulate you, because you are one of the top 1% of people on planet earth who actually has taken the time to seek out a new beginning and improve your situation. Most people are prepared to be played like pawns in the big game. They get up in the morning to the same old routine, get into work ,put in their shift, do what they are programmed to do, come home, put their feet up, watch television and go to sleep only to start the same old dreary routine again tomorrow morning and then wonder why they don't feel fulfilled in life.

Rich Man Poor Man:

I pull no punches in this book because life is too short to cheat yourself out of the quality of living you are entitled to, so now I'm going to lay it on you. The only reason you do not make as much money now as you say you want is because you are more comfortable with being poor than the idea of being rich. That's right I said it because it needed to be said. If you were comfortable with being rich you would be doing all the things that you need to do relentlessly to become rich. Instead you continuously justify your reasons for inaction and make excuses for not following through.

When it comes down to it, you lie to yourself and place imaginary and real obstacles in your way to prevent yourself from becoming rich because you don't believe you should have abundant wealth. Is it possible some of you don't believe you deserve to be rich because you have been indoctrinated by religion and culture not to be? Is it possible you have learned to accept being FILTHY rich is bad? Is possible your mind as a child was continuously assaulted by a general doctrine that rich people were not to be trusted; money was the root of all evil and that money cannot buy you happiness.

I am here to fly in the face of that kind of trash talk and state, money does buy you happiness. Money is heaven. Money is the root of joy and happiness. You can give, employ, empower, educate, free, teach and create an abundance of love with money. Would it be interesting to create an abundance of love within yourself and accept that you deserve to be rich just as much as anyone else? If you were to develop the habit of believing you deserve to have open access to the wealth that this wonderful earth provides, what would that be like? Do you believe you were born to this earth for a life of poverty and hardship? Or were you born with infinite capacity to think, create and become whatever you dream to become?

What is the immediate positive affect when you begin to fill your dreams with passion? Could it be you dream bigger dreams and dream more, because the more you dream, the more you desire. The more you desire, the more dissatisfaction you create. The more dissatisfaction you create the more action you will take. The more action you take the more you give. The more you give the more you receive. The more you receive the more you give and this is generally true.

There are few true obstacles on your path to success, almost all are your own self-imposed hurdles which you can tackle and dominate through personal growth. The rest of the challenges you meet and have latched onto as convenient excuses, are just that, convenient excuses. Remember, there is no challenge ever thought up by man that cannot be overcome by man.

Success and failure are not giant objects but an accumulation of action or inaction over a period of time. It's an accumulation of all those little successes over a given period and over a lifetime that gives us pride and joy in knowing that this life is our own to design and rule. If all you do is take action and improve, just 1% each day; what would the cumulative difference be over one year? The answer is; phenomenal and infinite. Anything that you focus on with continuous daily commitment and energy will improve, that's just a universal law like gravity is a universal law. See dissatisfaction as a beautiful gem and a motivating force because the more you can rouse your dissatisfaction, the easier you will find it to motivate change in the situation. Use that energy to submerge your mind within continuous progression and then great things will surface.

Get to the Upstairs of Your Mind.

You can come up with a billion dollar idea in the shower one morning, get on a plane, arrive in another country and you don't even have to pay any import duty. You don't even have to declare it and most don't. Some people never declare their ideas even to themselves and as a result they are broke, sick, tired and never go on to make any money. They stay poor and blame it on the conditions, economic, personal or otherwise because they are not in the habit of making decisions and acting on them. We are all bound and liberated by our decisions and the actions we take as a result of those decisions. Here's a news flash to the wise, if you have your own inspiration that FEELS like a great idea, then move on it, write it out, tease it out with all positivity. This is the Universe giving you go-fuel. Don't wait, act on it. The universe is acting as your cheerleader saying, go for it, time to do something, move it. Dump your restrictive beliefs and don't wait, take action. Learn to fine tune your intuition and listen to your own creativity more often.

You don't have to wait for the economy of Ireland or Europe or the world to turn around and you certainly can't sit and wait for politicians to change the conditions for your increased wealth. Remember the main reason you are either poor, broke or don't have enough money is you. That's right, you are to blame, not the outside forces, you are the biggest obstacle to your own success. You can sit around and wait for things to change, if you do, you will grow old, stay poor or die. If you're out of work, and don't have the money you need, then get into something that could provide an opportunity for wealth. The solution could be selling. Preferably sell in an area you love or have a hobby in. Choose a product or service you care about, have a passion for now or when you were a child. What do you have a passion for?

It doesn't matter who you are, where you're from or what your previous trade was. All people are continuously selling all day every day, they are just not aware of the situation they are in. Whether you recognize it or not, you have been selling and negotiating with your parents, siblings, friends, spouse and every person you have met since birth. In fact the reason you don't recognize that you are selling all of the time is because you have become unconsciously competent in the art. You have had a lifetime of practice in negotiating and selling, without being consciously aware. Whether negotiating at dinner or trying to persuade the children to go to a football game you are constantly selling all day every day. Do you recognise and accept this as fact?

If you know the right thing to say to get the kids to clean the car or get the wife to cook something special "that's selling". So why not get paid for something that you're already great at, you've had a lifetime of practice.

Whether you're a carpenter, bricklayer or a window cleaner, you have a bag of tools you use each day to get the job done, get paid and bring home the happy cash. In order to get that carpentry job, extension to build or windows to clean you had to sell yourself over and over again through the years. You had to sell yourself and the quality of the work. You sold the owners on their satisfaction to the point where they parted with their cash and were happy to do so.

You sold the suppliers on giving you a discount, better credit terms and the other trades on their negotiated rates. In fact you are continuously selling; you probably prefer not to recognize your actions as selling because it brings up negative connotations.

Isn't it a great feeling when a supplier offers you a 10% discount and you push and successfully negotiate for 15%. Doesn't that give you a great feeling of satisfaction when you walk out that door knowing you have an extra 50, 100, or 500 shekels in your pocket, and all this happened because you asked? That's selling, and you've been doing this all your life without even knowing. How does it actually feel, getting that little extra? Hold onto that feeling and we'll visit this area later.

If you are going to sell seriously, then you need to learn above all else, how to ask the right types of questions and how to close. It's your business to fill the sales funnel and that includes making cold calls, chasing leads, and following up on referrals. It is your duty, not just to yourself, but to your family and the dreams you have, to learn to close prospects sequentially and properly. These are just some of the actions that you learn and become consciously aware of as you generate business and put more money in your pocket. If you are going to sell professionally how important on a scale of one to ten do you think it is to be educated properly in the art of selling? Some people are not comfortable making cold calls; they have unjustified fears and lack of confidence, simply because they have not yet been equipped to do the job properly. Being able to develop your cold calling skills to a competency of confidence, effectiveness and professionalism will open infinite gates of opportunity where you feel in control. The direction you want to go in your life and your level of financial abundance are directly dependant on the enhancement of skills you already possess. If your business were a pair of black leather shoes, when was the last time you got polished and shined you shoes? How do the look, smell and feel after you've put a real shine on them?

CHAPTER 2

What do you see when you place an ant under a microscope?

Everything

Reframe Your Mind and Expect Success:

Unmotivated individuals make lousy salesmen and make no money. Let's face it; if you're not motivated to make a good living you're wasting your time and everybody else's. If you don't want an excellent standard of living and all the good things that go with financial abundance then why waste your time. Go find a nice corner and sit on your bum. On the other hand, if you have decided that you want to have the choice to be generous or not, if your decision is to be above the average played pawn on this planet and awaken the giant that nestles inside you, then welcome to the real world. You have taken the time to come forward and present you to yourself as your own guest speaker. You have made a choice to be the host of your own good fortune to leave behind the mundane general world and design your own particular self. As of this moment you are the creator of your own life, the Michelangelo of the David which is your future. You have the inherent genius inside you to model your life any way you wish. If you absolutely expect and believe that you will have success, then that is what you shall receive. If you absolutely expect and believe you will receive money, then that is what you will receive. Be specific, because whatever you concentrate on manifests through thought and continuous action.

Unfortunately there are so many people who expect rejection. They expect failure and that is their ultimate result. Happiness and sadness are both choices, one is pretty, the other ugly. Both are reflections of the same question with a different answer. One gives you a life of hardship, the other a life of comfort. One gives you disease; the other gives you good health and the ability to harvest that which you have planted. Your attitude and mindset are infectious.

Your prospects and the people you come into contact with know if you are congruent in your message. When you truly believe in what you are doing, people are more likely to be attracted to you and persuaded by your way of thinking. In the eyes of others and those around you, your status rises vertically and the heavenly harvest which you had previously sown becomes a light and cheerful chore.

In order to develop the correct attitude and mindset for your journey, develop a hunger within yourself, for it is the burn within you that is the motivation. How effective do you think it would be to teach yourself to motivate at will? By asking yourself the types of questions that push your own emotional buttons you can learn to do this. Start by asking yourself questions like," why is this thing I am doing important to me?" "What is it I am doing, that is so important?" The exercise is much more effective when you answer the questions on paper rather than just saying it to yourself because you activate the invisible force of your internal drive which is a most powerful motivating energy. The more reasons why, that you generate, the more you unearth feelings that align your reality to motivation. Ask yourself the question why is it you are concentrating and seeking those improvements in finances, family, education, spirituality, business and career? As you develop the habit of finding those answers your performance will increase. You need enough reasons to clarify what is most important to you, to the point where you can feel a physical wrench inside you.

Make it a part of your daily routine to continuously and intentionally court those interesting compliments that drive you on to the land of plenty.

In a nutshell, the reasons why you are doing what you are doing are most important because if you have enough reasons why, then you are sure to succeed. If you ask anyone why they failed their last project 99 times out of a hundred it was not from outside forces, it's because they did not have enough reasons why, hence a failure to motivate themselves to the level they needed to be at to succeed.

If you cannot afford to fail you then create motivation as a daily thirst. Just as you will die without water, your dreams will die without the correct motivation.

Ask yourself the types of questions that are so real it will sicken your stomach if you don't follow through. Ask deep questions that really hurt when you think of failing your wife and children or those you really care about, because these types of questions are seriously motivating and will certainly get your ball rolling.

Create a feeling of urgency. Ask why your actions are so important. Just as you develop a muscle in the gym, you will develop a self-realizing power to the point of where you say and totally believe "I can do, be and change anything I want" and you are launched into action.

On a day to day basis we get distracted and forget why we do what we do. If you want to develop that desire to succeed, it will take commitment and persistence on your part. You may ask, well how long will this take? My answer is "how bad do you want it".

An excellent way to get that correct leverage on yourself is asking the questions that bring your focus to "what's in this for me or my family?" Holding yourself to higher standards is hard if you don't have enough reasons to do so. Develop your passion; reside in the land of abundance, wealth, happiness, flow. Choose life and give yourself the fuel to take off. Emotion is the force of life and if you create enough positive emotion you will put yourself and those closest to you in a space that is happy, spontaneous, sincere and appreciative. People will stand back in awe and view the amazing blissful lifestyle you have created.

If you can teach yourself what drives you to action, the benefits are amazing. You can then contribute more to others by developing a prolific and confident understanding of how emotions motivate. When you understand the invisible forces that shape us you will become an effective communicator and leader, with an ability to consistently motivate others.
Expecting success is a crucial part of your success, but you must equip yourself for the journey by giving yourself the necessary tools to do the job.

Present Your Message

How you present what you are saying is vitally important. The pitch and tone of your speech are subconsciously monitored by those you are attempting to communicate with. The message you are attempting to communicate must match the intent within the message. The words you use and how you say them are directly linked to your proposal being accepted or not.

Imagine if you could master the art of communication. How would that impact your business?

Develop a courageous tone that is worthy of the diligent effort you have put in thus far to get you here. Why on earth would you want to blow it for lack of confidence? How you speak can be mastered by your own initiative in developing the way you say things. By thoughtful, deliberate practice you can master your skills to become a more effective communicator.

The pace at which you speak should be regularly monitored. If you are speaking with a prospect/ potential customers in the same language but have different accents, you need to slow down. Just because you understand your accent, that doesn't mean the prospect understands you. It's very annoying to a potential customer when they cannot understand what you are trying to convey. It's a lot easier for the prospect to say "I'm not interested", rather than, "please could you explain that to me one more time and by the way would you mind slowing down". What are the financial benefits to you when you can clearly convey your sales proposal? What are the negative impacts in several areas when you fail to create clarity with the prospect?

Create a Straw Man

Plan, prepare and practice relevant questions because they are vital for the sales process. If you don't have target questions for individual sales situations and have not practiced the objections associated with them your client is likely to come up with his own. If you don't handle those objections appropriately the prospect will sense a lack of confidence in your proposal and the result will likely be loss of the sale. How empowering do you think it feels to be able to rattle off a serious of open ended questions that your prospect feels obliged to answer?

Questions are vitally important because they focus the mind of your prospect. Planning, preparing and practicing questions are pivotal and it's what successful sales people repeatedly do. You don't need to reinvent the wheel, just copy the successful ones. Developing habits like these not only puts dollars in your pocket but increases your accuracy. When you have planned, prepared and practiced your confidence rises exponentially to the point where you know you can handle anything the prospect comes back with, giving you, the advantage in the sales situation. How do you think you will feel when you can close more opportunities than you lose?

Always build expansive open ended questions that give your prospects the opportunity to talk about and say what's really on their mind. Questions need to target the prospect on the things that you would like them to think about.

Real sales professionals are prepared, they have the proposal form already filled out, simply requiring the prospect's signature. The reason for this is twofold; they visualize the prospect signing, combining confidence with will. Just like the professional golfer or soccer player, they visualize the end result many times before they even step up to take the shot.

If you have asked the appropriate questions, handled all the objections and continually closed, getting enough minor yes answers, then getting the final authorization on the partially completed order form will be a lot smoother. Imagine getting paid over and over again, what could you spend the extra money on?

Have your tools to hand and not in your brief case, which means your authorization form should be filled out as much as possible and you must have a pen to hand during the presentation. You look unprofessional and give off that signal when you start having to fumble, looking for a pen or an authorization form. Organized, prepared, professionals ooze confidence. They expect success, work out what tools they need for the presentation beforehand and close with confidence. You can do this if you really want to. How bad do you want it?

Top producers always have an authorization form filled out on the table and several blanks in their brief case because It's what real sales professionals do. Do you want to be one of the top 20% in your industry who make 80% of the money, or do you want to be in the 80% of losers who share 20% of the money? It is your choice.

Switch OFF Your Phone!

Never take a live phone into a sales situation unless it is required. Divert all calls, silence the message alert system and give your prospect the one hundred per cent attention they deserve, after all, you have made the effort to get the appointment. It's not only discourteous, it also hints of disorganization. Would you like to blow the presentation by being interrupted for something trivial like someone asking you out to lunch? When you are interrupted during the sales process both the prospect and your attention are diverted. It could happen at a crucial point in the meeting. You will likely botch the close, lose the client and lose the sale. You're smarter than that, don't take the chance.

CHAPTER 3

Can't see the wood from the trees?

Set Your Objectives

Without planning a clear set of objectives for the day you are wasting the most precious commodity that you have, your valuable time. That's right; time is valuable and they're not making any more of it. You should have the night before a detailed breakdown of the available work time translated into how much money you would like to earn, per day, per hour, per minute, because it's only when you start accurately measuring your time in minutes that you get to value the importance of time and a true picture of your productivity emerges. Wow, what a concept, imagine if you actually had your time measured and it became abundant because of your action, what level of certainty would that give you? Imagine if you had certainty throughout your day. Would that give you more stress or less stress?

In order for you to improve and grow, set simple attainable targets and stick to them. By measuring things, you gain certainty and peace of mind.

Clarity promotes productivity and prevents poverty. Remember it's all about clarity. The clearer the picture you create in your mind and the more you visualize the outcome in detail, the more successful you will be. It's so simple.

Know why you are doing what you are doing and what's in it for you. If you were to continuously remind yourself of the future rewards for your efforts, where would your mind be focused? What do you think the effect on the task at hand would be?

When you are making prospecting calls, never put your phone down and always wear a headset because your appointment conversion ratio improves significantly. You will find it is most productive to keep that positive energy you have flowing. When you are in that groove, you will want to stay there as long as possible. Putting down and picking up the phone for every call not only wastes time but also saps your mental energy. It is certainly true, while using a hand held phone you are more likely to become distracted and start taking longer and longer breaks. Be smart, wear the headset and see your appointment scheduling increase. If you could increase your appointment ratio by ten, twenty or thirty per cent just by using a different tool, how would that effect your bank balance? By how much would you like to increase your profit?

The Scary Theory

Contrary to public opinion, sales, is not a numbers game. There used to be an old adage in all the sales books that you make 30 calls to get three appointments and hence close one sale or similar ratios. Back then and still in some places today, sales managers measured the number of calls sales persons made, divided it into time and then divided it into dollars. That was all well and good to have the office statistics to figure out the office running costs but what I believe happened was these numbers were passed on to sales people in sales training. Sales numbers like this were banded about and then a dollar figure was put on each call. So if a commission was 600 dollars on an item, product or service then each call was worth 600 / 30 calls = 20 dollars earned per call, or if it took 20 calls to gain 3 appointments then the value of each appointment is 200 dollars

If you are a newly hired sales person and a sales manager tells you the overall office statistic of 30 calls per 3 appointments per one sale! Well that's what you are going to believe. That new belief becomes your reality. You need to understand they are overall office statistics and nothing related to individual sales persons with different ratios. That's all fine and dandy to motivate yourself to make the calls, if you have lots of time and just like making sales calls hoping a sale will come. Hoping is not good enough. I used to think the same way and I operated like that until one day while having a shower I had an idea suddenly hit me like a truck and it goes like this: Each call you make is worth the full commission!

That's right, if the commission is 600 or 1000, or 200, then each phone call you make is worth to you, or going to cost you 600, or 1000, or 200 if you fail to secure the appointment. You see it's only when you change your own psychology to the point of, "I call it confident panic", that you realize the seriousness of the excellent opportunity you have been given. If you understand that every time you lose an appointment on the phone it costs you 1000 Euro or 1000 dollars whichever your currency, it takes on a whole new meaning. If I said to you "well you blew that one, you just cost yourself 20 euro", well you and most other mediocre sales people could live with that. What if you were to start saying to yourself: "I just blew that potential appointment because I had not prepared properly and it cost me a thousand euro that I needed for school fees" or "I just blew that potential appointment because I had not prepared properly and it cost me a thousand euro that I needed for my daughters new dental work" Now it takes on a whole new weight. Now you sit up and notice, because this is beyond serious. Now you sit up and say to yourself "I better turn the next one around". Why do you think you begin to react with a different outlook?

The reason is pain; because the pain you have just created gives you emotional leverage on yourself. By getting to the core of why you are doing what you are doing you unleash great motivating powers that are lying dormant inside you.

Now here is the good news!

This is just the beginning for you. This is just a tiny fraction of the self-motivating powers you possess. Recognizing and accepting the fact that you have infinite potential can be very scary for some people, plus the fact that it is non-quantifiable and it's free. How awesome is it that you have this unlimited infinite ability to change your world and the world of those around you just by tapping into a tiny percentage of your brain and creating leverage using something that you have complete control over?

I'm here to dispute those outdated sales psychology books. I have tested the scary theory on myself and it works. You can slash those old sales ratio numbers and get a huge measurable boost if you have enough emotional leverage to give you the power, passion and motivation to succeed.

If you can create emotion that scares the hell out of you to the point of 'I cannot' and 'I refuse to fail', your sales numbers will skyrocket exponentially because you have created motivation through leverage. On the other hand, if you continue to go down the old path of the numbers game and burn off leads, you will not have learned or earned, and your days will certainly be long. If you don't change you will probably blow the opportunity for the additional earnings that could have paid for the children's education, holidays, or new clothes for the wife. How do you think you are going to feel about that?

If you could halve the ratio of rejection phone calls and presentations by scaring the hell out of yourself would you? What would the result be? Now you are still fresh for the day and you've saved yourself 20 hours a week on the phone, 80 hours a month that you could be spending with your kids or 960 hours per year to play golf, vacation or whatever blows your hair back, how do you think an accomplishment like that would feel?

That's right. You can save yourself almost a thousand hours a year in phone calls that you shouldn't be making in the first place, just by taking a new approach and realizing the serious consequences of doing what you are doing and the penalties for not sufficiently motivating yourself. So go ahead, scare the bejesus out of yourself to the point of obsession where you refuse to fail. Don't listen to the nega-tatoes of this world, the coffee pot junkies with no sales on the board, the let me take you under my wing merchants who once tried to fly but crashed and burned in their own heroic sad little world. Stay away from those people. Hang with the 20 % who make 80% of the sales and the money. Surround yourself with positivity and positive emotional leverage as the world stands back in awe of your achievement.

Physiology and Success

When you beam an amazing energetic approach your prospects are influenced. The way you use your physiology is a key ingredient in the combination of tools that contribute to your wealth. I cannot stress enough to sales individuals, the importance of mastering this tool not only as a subconscious self-motivator but as a ratchet for disarming the toughest prospects. If you come across as pleasant, poised and jovial you are far more likely to relax the client.

How you use your body language, posture, facial expressions and breathing can bring a fresh and friendly approach to a tense situation. Having awareness and being able to change your physiology gives you instant control over your mental state. Prospects can tell just by the way you are sitting , standing, talking or moving, whether you are up for the situation or not. How you use your body language sends signals to others about where you are coming from and whether you can be trusted.

Word Power

Awesome, incredible, fantastic, brilliant, exponential, glorious, happy, satisfied, genius, unlimited, these are the types of words I love because they resonate with power. Your choice of words and how you use them can move mountains.

You can persuade a prospect to your way of thinking simply by using certain words. If you take the word " BECAUSE" it is a cause/effect word and it can be used to get people to think and react in different scenarios. Human beings always want to have a reason to explain an event, a theme, excuses or a success. Sometimes you may hear a statement similar to" it was a bad game because the ref wouldn't let the game flow" or "it was a great game because the conditions were perfect". If you take the word "because" to its inception in your life, you were either denied or rewarded according to the word. "Mammy can I have an ice cream", "No", "Please Mammy can I have an Ice cream", "No BECAUSE you are going to bed shortly and ice cream keeps you awake". End of discussion and you became programmed to accept the cause/effect inference.

It has been proven that a higher percentage of people will go ahead with your proposal when you use the word BECAUSE. Studies by behavioral specialists have shown that you can increase your conversion ratios if you can manage to utilize the word BECAUSE into your conversation effectively.

Another word you became programmed with from infancy was the word "NOW",if you were requested to do something by your parents and you didn't want to do it, after a bit of debate back and forward , with tonality your parent would say do it "NOW" and that would be pretty much the end of the argument. The word 'now' can also be used with a much softer tone as if a matter of fact, i.e. "I really want you to do this 'Now' " and continue on with rest of the sentence. This word will be subconsciously received just as the word BECAUSE and you will get a higher level of cooperation. Word power is an awesomely effective sales tool which you may wish to investigate BECAUSE it will help you increase your bottom line. I'm not saying you should do it NOW but you may wish to make a note and do it when you are ready to earn more money.

Chapter 4

Your Amazing Exponential Potential

What are Gods renowned for? How about, creating things out of nothing? Because you are part God and already possess the ability to create something out of nothing, let's say, thought for example, then don't you think it's possible you could create your own universe the way you want it?

If you are thinking about getting into the unlimited wealth, building profession of selling, then sell only those things you are really interested in. Sell only Items that you love looking at, talking about and have a real genuine interest in. That's right, it could even be a service or a hobby. I state this because you will be far more enthusiastic, knowledgeable and genuine about the product. Prospects will feel your infectious enthusiasm which will lead to an easier accumulation of sales and happy pay days for you that will grow exponentially.

Never forget: A prospect can spot you coming a mile down the tracks. If you don't believe in your product and the welfare of the purchaser, you may make the occasional sale, but you will never reach the level of sales you might aspire to. It is much easier to sell something you are genuinely interested in and it will show in your bank balance.

As you acquire new skills, be a gentle giant. Never try to rough ride someone into a sale that is not in their best interest just so you can make a commission. If you develop that bad habit, the likely result will be loss of sales, clients, your credibility and that of your firms. That's how an unprofessional operates. If it's not in the customer's best interest and it's not a win-win situation for both parties, find an alternative or decline to offer. What type of reputation and how much respect could you earn by going the extra mile for your customers in creating a win-win situation for both of you in every transaction?

A True Story

I once had a customer called Bill who qualified for a home purchase well in excess of a million dollars. He was a very particular and meticulous man and for a living he read large reinsurance insurance contracts worth hundreds of millions of dollars. He wanted that multimillion dollar feeling but wanted to purchase a home for between 700,000 and 900,000 dollars. Over a period of six months he put in 3 separate contracts, on three separate homes, and backed out of all three before the attorney review period was over. He would always find some reason for doing so, like the sound of distant traffic late at night, or a power line at the end of the field in the school where his children would be attending. It was enough to give him cause for concern. I did mind him pulling out of the contracts and it was a bit frustrating for me but he had a genuine belief in his own concerns. Though I could empathize with his objections I had to respect his beliefs to a point and I was unsuccessful in finding his family the home in the area that I serviced. I didn't see him for a while, even though I kept in regular contact. I even went door to door in a couple of developments he liked to enquire if anyone would be willing to sell. After a couple of months I got a call from Bill saying that he had bought a new build forty miles away from where we had been looking. My lost prospect did give the selling realtor my card but he chose not to honor the referral system and as a result I lost a partial commission. I was a bit taken aback momentarily but I wished Bill and his family all the best and I was happy they had found their home. I genuinely didn't mind at this stage because I had a funny feeling something good would come from my efforts. As a result Bill and I went out and had a few beers and struck up a genuine close friendship. I really came to love the guy. Bill could never understand why I didn't get annoyed with him and to this day we are good friends. He later said to me the fact that I didn't try to sell him something he didn't want, and I didn't keep pushing him gained me a lot of respect in his book. As a result of our interaction and my caring about his family, he introduced me to some of his buddies who were in the market for homes. I gladly serviced their needs, made more than the money I thought I had lost and benefitted by making a whole bunch of new friends.

The business point I wish to make is, if I had of taken more time qualifying Bill's needs, wants and aversions I could have saved lots hours of driving Bill and his wife around looking at houses they should not have been looking at, and writing contracts that I should not have been writing.

The moral point of the story is, in order to succeed you need to steer away from the false, promote the true, and as you brighten your life the flower that is you will unfold. You become an awesome power by the strong roots you have sown. As the foolish sink they are held captive by the restrictions in their own minds, while the wise few float and are liberated. For the fortunate are ready to give and ready to walk an extra mile with a man just for the kindness of the act. They are not stingy with their time or their empathy. They are not gloomy and sad, but a joy to be around. Generous and cheerful they give more than they receive, and in return they become great and grow past the shrinking unimportant hosts of negativity.

First Impressions are so Important

Whether you are calling someone on the phone or door stepping a potential client, how you look, sound and communicate in the first 20 seconds can generally make or break the sale. You need to plan, prepare and practice your opening statement so it is received in the manner of interest you wish it to be.

The more preparation and practice you do, the more appealing and confident you will feel. You need to ooze the confidence that can only come with consistent rehearsal and experience. I cannot emphasize enough the importance of role play and practicing your opening statement. There is a limit on the time you have to get your message across to the prospect. How do you think it might feel to get more positive reactions than rejections? What would that do for your confidence?

In that first twenty seconds the prospect wants to know, as he thinks consciously or subconsciously, 1 who are you, 2 what do you want, 3 why should I listen to you and 4 what's in it for me.

You need to be more than, "Well it's just about this, or just about that". Never use the phrase in an early sales opening, "well it's just about this or that product". Come across as being clear, exact and confident in your tone, pitch and presence. You must put yourself above the average sales person and you must fully believe it in your heart and soul. There can be no partial absence on your part, you must create a presence. "I'm here, I'm exact, I know what I'm talking about and I'm here to help you".

Remember this is the way forward in creating abundance in your life. By refusing to accept that you are average you can change your own economy. It cannot be accidental, it must be intentional that through your own will and desire you are bringing forth the energy, talents and power that you have within you.

Chapter 5

The Five Tributaries of Wealth

What you are about to read are the fundamentals of all business. You have already proven to be remarkable by having the foresight to purchase this book for your further advancement and you may wish to pay particular attention to the next few sections. How thriving can it be to have an actual simple proven formula to increase your profits? What do you think the feeling would be like if you knew you had that knowledge in your hand? The founder of the number one business coaching franchise in the world, Action Coach, shows how to use this formula as a basic for incremental business growth. His name is Bradley Sugars and I have adapted some of Brad's teachings to suit my simple presentation to you. Thanks Brad, you're a genius.

To increase your profits there are 5 areas of your business you need to concentrate on. I like to call it Kaizen through the five tributaries. The principal relates to the continuous incremental improvement in five areas of the business that you can control. Those areas are lead generation, conversion rate, repetitive transactions, average sale price and margins. By making small changes in these areas month on month or week on week you can create a cumulative effect of exponential growth. I am not saying it will be easy because change can be more difficult for some, but if you are truly ready for positive change, trust yourself and trust the system. The more you acclimatize yourself to change, the easier it flows and benefits increase.

Your lead generation is the most important of the five steps because it relates to the total amount of enquiries you receive through intentional marketing or by accident. EVERYTHING FLOWS FROM YOUR LEAD GENERATION. Almost all challenges in every business can be overcome by converting leads into sales and directing that cash into a challenged area wisely. Leads can come in the form of a walk in, walk by, telephone enquiry or any amount of infinite techniques or styles of marketing. There are no rules in this area but one, do whatever works for you. Consider and create a style that makes you stand out and get noticed.

What do you think are some of the rewards of being consistent and growing renewed green shoots in this area?

Are the benefits limited or are they exponential?

Why? Take a moment and think about this.

Your conversion rate is the percentage of those hard earned enquiries that you convert into customers.

If you were to be honest with yourself, on a scale of 1 to 10 how enthusiastic do you think you should be to learn to convert the highest percentage of those leads into sales?

What are the financial benefits to your business, your family and you?

What are some of the challenges you could overcome in your business with additional cash flow?

If you were to master what you should be mastering anyway, what could you do with the additional income?

If you know you can, then why haven't you?

What sort of pain do you feel when you don't have enough cash?

How much pleasure do you feel when your wallet is stuffed with bank notes?

What does it feel like when you know you can just buy stuff?

Who do you love that you can give to?

Your conversion rate works as follows: 1000 enquiries x 30% = 300 customers converted. So your conversion rate is equal to 30%. That is a pretty dismal conversion rate but that's where you are and always will be until you learn to qualify your prospects, ask the right types of questions, close and sell properly.

Repetitive transactions, represents the number of times you can convince each customer to do business with you in a year.

If it were more productive to sell to only new customers rather than repeat customers, then we would be doing that all the time?

Contrary to that, once you have converted a prospect, it is usually far more efficient and less expensive to sell to a customer repeatedly than a prospect because the customer has already purchased and probably likes and trusts you in most cases.

When you maintain a kind and friendly relationship with your customers, what is the likelihood they will do business with you again?

If they like and trust you, are they more likely or less likely to go searching somewhere else?

When you calculate the monthly, annual, or lifetime sales value of each customer, what does that add up to?

How important do you think it might be to know those numbers?

Because you are now more knowledgeable, with what vigour should you implement strategies to retain your customers and get them to purchase more often?

Your average sale price represents the monetary addition of all the transactions divided by the number of transactions. Innovative business leaders know the numbers in their field because without having a handle on your numbers it's hard to lift that pot of gold. Knowing the average sale price per product, service or offering allows you the vison of raising the revenue to a sustainable acceptable level. Raising the average sale price by just five per cent doesn't even get noticed on lots of products but has a huge cumulative effect along with additional other measures on the profitability of your businesses.

If you were enthusiastic and did believe it was possible to raise your average sale price even in an economic downturn, what percentage would you raise it by?

300 customers x (transactions) 8 times per year x (average sale price) 76Euro = 182,400 Turnover.

Margin is the amount you have left after all expenses. It is absolutely amazing that people will invest their own money and end up working 60 to 80 hours per week in a small business for 0 to 10 per cent margin, sometimes not paying themselves and then become resistant to change that situation through growth and positive steps. There are at least 60 different recognised methods to increase your margins and there are infinite variations and combinations of methods in completing the same task.

If you were to be just a little bit brave and apply your aptitude, how delighted would you feel to see your margin climb month after month after month?

If you were to equip yourself with the knowledge of how to increase your margins incrementally over time, what is the likelihood you would maintain a robust healthy appetite for more business?

Being incredibly optimistic with your scenario at this moment your margin is at 20%, so the actual profit is 182,400 x .20 = 36,480. Unfortunately those figures are not typical of a successful small business in Ireland today. They are 10% or less - you do the math and then ask yourself, what am I willing to do? And what's going to happen if I don't master these five critical areas of my business?

If you are smart enough to begin making tiny little improvements in the five key areas week on week, month on month, the business begins growing and accumulating exponentially. As little as a 10% increase in all five areas year on year for two years has a serious effect on your business and profits can be doubled at a minimum, even trebled because everything is cumulative.

Year 1

1000 x 1.1 x .33 = 363 customers x 9 x 83.6 = 273,121 x 22% = 59,866 profit.

Year 2

1100 x 1.1 = 1210 x 10 x 91= 1,101,100 turnover x .24% = 264,264 euro profit. That's a net increase of 227,784 over 2 years. This system works on all businesses because of the cumulative effect, but it doesn't work by itself. It requires immediate and dedicated action on your part to consistently monitor, test, measure and incrementally improve in all five tributary areas of growth. The possibilities are limitless if you implement the system.

You will find an abundance of wealth building strategies in this book guaranteed to increase your profits if you take the time to learn and use them. The questions I have implanted for you are designed to get you to think and they demand to be answered in a success journal daily.

What do you think would be the effect on your income if you answered questions such as these about your business and your life on a daily basis?

Well how much do you want and how bad do you want it?

If you could double your business in 12 months and work fewer hours just by working smarter, how would that affect your family, your finances, your outlook, your health?

It's your life, your choice and your decision. How you speak to yourself and answer these questions will have a direct effect on your life, your business, your family and your relationships.

Imagine you could have a successful business that gave you the quality of life that you dreamed of. How would it look?

If you could see your business paying you a substantial cheque every week that covered your bills and you could take two or even three full holidays a year while working less than 40 hours per week with flexible time, how successful would you feel?

The quality of your life is directly related to the quality of the questions you ask yourself and how you answer them on a daily basis. That's just basic universal law, just as gravity is a basic universal law. You can choose to work with or against universal law but remember swimming against a strong current is not advisable because eventually you will sink, as will your business. Whereas growing in the flow is refreshing, reassuring and healthy.

Chapter 6

The Mechanics of Your Business

In the previous section we have being talking about the 5 areas of your business. Here are the areas you have complete control over again, lead generation, conversion of leads to sales, number of transactions per customer per time period, average sale price per customer and your profit margins. You need to understand, these areas of the business are completely influenced by your actions and the decisions that you take. It is that simple; you can take control and derive certainty of profit in your business if you influence the following subjects in a positive incremental fashion. It all comes down to you.

How important is it for you to take control of your own destiny?

Because you actually have choice now, what level would you like to take your earnings to?

Here are some alternate tips for generating leads and filling the sales funnel. I am not saying any one strategy is better than the next. The idea here is to open your mind to the possibility that there are an infinite and undeterminable number of effective lead generation measures. The challenge is to find some that are efficient, effective and suit your business, because they all work. The secret is mastery of one or two methods over time and then adding to them as you master the next. It is important to be patient and not start jumping from one method to the next until you have mastered the technique.

Facebook has at present 2.4 billion users and growing - imagine that. If you are not using this free instantaneous vehicle for marketing your business, then get over your fears and start mastering the number one store in the world. Learn to control what you can control and become a master at exposing your business. Your bank balance will love you for it.

Door Stepping: I find it effective and I always gain a considerable amount of qualified leads. You don't know who you are going to meet, what sort of a mood they might be in or what's going on in their business. If you learn to love door stepping, like it's relish, your days can be amazing.

Think of it this way, you have power to be a true alchemist, that is, change people's universe just by the things you say and the positive attitude you display. It's an awesome feeling of power to have the ability to influence people and make them happy. Not only can you positively influence your prospects but it also has a ripple effect on the people who they interact with throughout their day.
I find it beneficial to have an ice breaker that will get some attention. I can think of some of the most outlandish things to say on the spot to get someone's attention. I shock them and then tell them I'm only joking. The result is a big sigh of relief and then a laugh. It works every time for me.

School Newsletter Ads: If you are a local trader or small business, then this type of advertisement can be very effective for you because you are investing in a small captive audience. The advertisement space is usually inexpensive; it gives the appearance of an endorsement by the school, which we know is not true but it adds credibility and trust for your business in the local environment. It's an easy way to connect with the local population and you will be delighted with the incremental benefit of that additional turnover. Remember it's all about making small cost effective changes that become accumulative over time.

Press releases: This is free advertising which your bank balance loves. The article needs to be almost print ready. If your story is likely to grab the reader's attention it's likely to grab the journalist's attention and get printed. If you were to try and build a profile by becoming a regular contributor how do you think that would affect your business? Be consistent and don't give up until you succeed. Rejection is just fuel for the future.

Database Lists: You can buy them or build them. If you consider the amount of time it takes to build a data base it may be more economical to purchase a database but you've got to be careful as to the obvious - accuracy, age, target and usage. On the other hand a newly built database may be more accurate, targeted and virgin. You could also go into the municipal library where you will find an abundance of lead generating information and library attendants who are so kind and more than happy to help you. Let's have a big cheer for the librarians. What are the benefits to your endeavours of striking up a friendly relationship with your local librarian?

Direct Mail: Specifically targeted direct mail to the prospect that creates an interest pre-announcing a phone call, and then following up, is another masterful way to generate prequalified leads. Use the first few words to sell and write as if you are actually talking to that person. Use positive refreshing language and don't forget the P.S. at the end because it's an effective seller.

Collaborative Invoice Mailing: If you have a relationship with another non-competing business you could piggyback their monthly invoice system with an advertisement insert that is great for their customers. This technique appears to give your host the credit for the offer which pleases them. You could also try an endorsed letter of referral from your host partner and again you deflect credibility to the host even though the two companies are working together.

Building Signage: Bright and colourful with a powerful selling headline that faces both ways in traffic. Are you a secret agent? What are some of the negative effects if no one else knows where you are? How much will that cost you financially? What are some of the positive effects if everyone who passes by notices your sign? If you could think of a few outrageous ideas to get noticed, what would they be?

Car Signage: Try placing three bold and bright magnetic stick on mats on your vehicle with a selling headline advertising your product or service and phone number. Place two on the sides and one on the back. It's free advertising and a no brainer. What is the one thing you can put on the sign that will get you noticed? What does it cost your business financially every time you drive when you are not being noticed versus how much money does it make you when you are being noticed? It's pretty easy to calculate. Trusting you require accurate information to grow your business, how effective would it be if you were to ask your prospects each time they called where they heard of you?

Sidewalk Signage: It doesn't have to be your sidewalk. It can be anywhere as long as it does not create an obstacle. Realtors normally put out 2-3 open house signs. I would put out 16 – 20 over a 2-3 mile area, hence I would always have a full open house and I would always sell my properties, usually on the first day. I was energized to encourage traffic to my offering. Skilled use of simple effective signs with a novel idea that gets noticed, banks you money. The sign can be a butchers sign up at the next corner or whatever your trade or business is. Use catchy colours, fonts and headlines with an offer that draws the observer to want to investigate further. Again, what can you put on your sign that is different and will get you noticed?

Networking: Events, parties, functions, trade shows or meet ups. Wherever there are people, it is incumbent on you to network, unless you don't like money. I am always networking and always getting new business from network events. Dress for business at all times because you never know who you are going to meet when you are out. Always carry a bunch of cards and always expect to do business wherever you go. Spend more time listening than talking as you qualify the other person. Do not waste your time following up with people who did not qualify, put them into your monthly newsletter email and let them mature. Always follow up the qualifiers by phone within 3 days. If you were a little more intuitive and took some measures to become more time efficient what would be the cumulative benefits of your actions?

Host Promotion: This is where you get permission to promote yourself to another businesses clients. It could be that you offer to pay part or some of the meeting room costs or give gifts in the hosts name to the attendees. You might offer to pay for the promotional mail out. It's important to have the host business endorse you and that their customers fall into your target market. Again it's all about preliminary qualification. If the shoe doesn't fit, the shoe doesn't fit. However if it does, you have a captive market with a warm introduction and an element of trust. This helps promote your product or service. Strategic alliances like this work when both parties understand the benefits to each other's business and are jointly motivated to action.

Referrals: The best types are previous customers because it helps them validate their purchase decision to their friends, family or business associates. They are inexpensive, effective and already carry a perceived level of trust.

If a friend recommended a supplier to you, how much more would you be willing to listen to the proposal because it came from someone you trusted rather than a stranger who just knocked on your door?
You receive referrals with ease after you have created exceptional value and service but you can also use and gain a referral as a closing tool by asking for one before you give the price. After you have almost completed your strategic presentation and just as you come to the compensation part you ask, Mrs Doyle my business is built on my reputation and the referrals I receive from happy customers just like you. Who do you know that would be interested in a fabulous kitchen just like yours? Mrs Doyle is likely to perceive she will get a better deal by giving you the referral and that may be the case or not. Mrs Molloy is likely to be highly impressed after receiving an enthusiastic phone call about her new kitchen from her good friend Mrs Doyle.
How positive is that referral?
What's the likelihood of getting a sale with Mrs Molloy if she's in the market for a new kitchen?
Reciprocal referrals with other businesses and generosity to loyal referral agents are additional strategies which may be used to boost qualified leads.

Telemarketing: You can learn to master this activity and generate qualified leads or you can outsource it. The benefits of outsourced versus in house is time, which is your most valuable asset. Out sourcing the function can be expensive but the numbers are what count. If the number of qualified leads from outsourced telemarketing generates an acceptable margin, then the number is exponential and it just makes sense. Outsourced services like this need to be consistently tested, measured and spot checked.

Cold Calling: some people say they don't like cold calling, well, I'm sorry but it's just an essential part of your business so get over it and learn to be competent. How is anyone going to become a warm call unless you heat them up? If you equip yourself with the right types of tools and enough reasons to do what you do, then cold calling does not feel like a task but becomes a joy and a genuine wealth builder. Cold calling can become an excellent money generator just by starting to make one new call a day building it to two the next day and three the next to four the next day and so on. By building your cold calling muscle over several months you become a true sales champion. If the product or service you are marketing has an end value of say three thousand euro, how motivated could you become with every phone call, knowing you can make three thousand euro or it will cost you three thousand euro based on the success or failure of the call?

You now have a few of the unlimited choices available to market your product or service. Whichever strategy you choose to suit, it is important to remember, incremental improvement brings you where you want to go. If you expect it to happen suddenly, then think again. It may take 3 to 6 months to become proficient at any one marketing strategy but the amount of time it takes is entirely dependent on your motivation, commitment, drive and passion to make more money.

Most marketing strategies will work but you must choose which ones are most suitable for your business. Unfortunately there are people who avoid success because they fail to focus. They try a marketing strategy for a week and when they see it's not working immediately, move on to other methods aimlessly wandering around the desert of no euro looking for an oasis. Test and measure the effectiveness of your chosen method over a period of time. It is imperative you or your staff ask every customer where they heard about your business. By asking the right types of questions you can tell which method is working and discover what you need to do to improve the flow. With a combination of various tested and proven methods over time you will be able to continuously replenish your prospects.

If you were to concentrate on the mastery of some selected marketing methods instead of jumping aimlessly from one system to the next ask yourself what would the benefits and effects in the areas of time, labour, costs, margins and profits be?

Chapter 7

Increasing Your Conversion Rate

When it comes to converting leads, you must remember, you have made nothing until you convert. No sale, no money, nothing. There are an infinite number of techniques you can use to help you to help others attain their needs and wants. Your job is to aid those people who have a desire for your product or service to get over their own resistance, by skilfully asking the right types of questions that allow the prospect to make their own decision that is a benefit for them. I have included in this chapter a sample of ideas to help you convert those prospects into customers. No one technique is the master of converting prospects into customers but with a combination of ideas you can help prospects make their own informed decisions on which product or service to purchase. It's only when they have been converted from a prospect to a customer by way of a financial transaction that you get paid. If you were to investigate, implement, track and measure the increased sales because you installed some additional conversion systems into your business, how much would it increase your revenue? If you had a feeling that better conversion techniques would increase your cash turnover, would you want to wait, or do you think it would be wise to get on that immediately?

Sales Scripts: An absolutely essential tool for every sales person or business owner. If you want impressive sales figures then progress to always using an innovative sales script. Your closure rate will double when a prepared and polished presentation or closure sequence is used to help the prospect value your proposition. The masterful development and use of an effective sales script will skyrocket your earnings as you convert properly qualified prospects.

Sales scripts should be a continuous series of open ended questions that lead the potential customer forward, allowing them to feel as if he or she is making an informed and intelligent decision. Have scripts for all occasions, all types of customers and insist on all of your staff using them.

Define what is novel about your product or service excluding price and quality. Be specific and say it effectively. Being different gets you attention and that's vital.

A Testimonial List: Skilfully use testimonials from happy customers beside a list of benefits to champion your product or service. Help prospects imagine the purchase decision by showing they were not the first to purchase your product. It also helps to demonstrate how the benefits positively affected other buyers.

Easy Purchase: Make it easy for customers to pay in cash, cheques, credit cards and bit coin. I am mentioning bit coin because it is here already and those who fail to adapt will lose a percentage of sales in the future depending on how stubborn you are to change. Be flexible and accept progress.

Reproduce Positive Print: If you have some favourable press articles relating to your business, then use them in your sales presentation or pre-sales kit. Hang them on the walls of your waiting room or office. Mailed or sent as part of the presales information package, they provide the customer with more confidence in their decision about the appointment. If you are using it as part of your actual sales presentation, it lends credibility. Focus the prospect there momentarily by a series of related questions. It's another tool to help move them forward and inspire confidence in their positive decision.

Use Questionnaires: You can fit a customer's needs more precisely by using a well-crafted questionnaire. It benefits all parties by introducing a deeper level of clarity which helps the buyer express specifically what they are looking for. Ultimately it makes the purchase decision easier.

Building Trust and Rapport: As you become more competent in learning how to develop trust and rapport earlier in the relationship the easier you will find your sales position. People will buy products more often and enjoy the experience of doing business with you when they feel they have developed a bond. It is your job as a business owner or sales person to acquire the skills necessary to build that trust because without it you will struggle on every sale. Trust and rapport are the fundamental building blocks of any sale, which is built on listening more than you speak, asking the right types of questions and acknowledging the customers concerns.

Using the latest Techniques: As a business owner how important might it be to learn how other people think, communicate and make decisions?
I believe it is essential to acquire such tools as neuro linguistic programming and other enhanced human communication products that give you the edge over your competition. You need to help yourself by taking the time to research what is available and what works for you.

Shifting Focus: If your prospect is stalling and not moving forward in the sales process it's probably because there is an objection you have not uncovered due to lack of clarity. Your client has not communicated the objection because you have failed to ask the appropriate qualifying questions. You may wish to turn their attention to a different model. If the stall is on price then show a

cheaper model. If it's on quality, then go to a higher price model, or go to colour. Test and measure with alternate choice probing questions until the true objection is uncovered, then go back at it with a test close and keep closing until you see the cash because you don't get paid until you close. A young sales person might ask, *"how many attempts should I make before it's a bit too much"?*
The answer is, as many as it takes to get paid. Never stop closing with questions until the money is in the till.

Asking for the Sale: it is amazing how many sales people go through all the prep work, the prospecting, setting the appointment, practicing, rehearsing the sales presentation, presenting the sales presentation and after all that work, fail miserably, simply because they lose their bottle in the final stages of the close. They become emotionally uncomfortable in that space between asking for the money and receiving the authorization because they have not mastered the key area of closing and have no repertoire of assumptive and alternate closes that lead the prospect gently to make the decision and take action. Assume the sale and apply the appropriate pressure to allow your prospect receive the product or service they came in for in the first place. The only reason they are not going forward is that you are standing in the way with your own incompetence and lack of closing power because you didn't take the time to equip yourself with the tools of your trade.

Guarantee: If you are using one it's a no brainer because it transforms doubt and uncertainty to trust and action by offering a no nonsense money back guarantee with your product or service. Find the key scare feature prospects have prior to purchase and neutralize it with the promise you will fix it if it goes wrong. Make sure your promise and guarantee is on your signage, business cards, documentation and products. Ensure you empower your staff to implement the guarantee in your absence, but never promise more than you can deliver. Make sure you advertise it and say it so people can hear your message.

Chapter 8

Repeat Business Strategies

The more you can get them to come back, the more you will enjoy your trips to the bank.

It takes much more effort and is far more expensive in time and money to get a new customer to purchase rather than an old one. Consider the life time cash value of a customer, what does it add up to? If you are convinced it is wise to target your past and ongoing customers, then you may wish to implement some of the basic strategies below. If you don't get your past customers to come back, how will that affect your business? What if you do get your customers to repeat several times per year- how will that affect your cash flow? The following are but a few of the many different ways to gain repeat business. Some are more effective for different types of businesses but they all work. Would it be wise to study them and make the incremental changes that will increase your cash flow? If you had a specific target what would be the percentage increase you would like to achieve over the next twelve months?

Dominate the Space: Your customer has a certain amount of mental space for any particular item, service or personality. Your job is to be at the forefront of that customer's mind so that whenever they think of a new or additional purchase in your market area, you are there. How powerful can a strategy like this be and what can it do for your sales? By taking consistent action you can dominate clients' subconscious space for your products or services either through email, text, telephone, networking or whatever method you prefer as long as you are always in touch or within easy reach. You can do that covertly or brazenly depending on how well you know the customer. It doesn't really matter what method you use as long as you do it. What is the alternative if you don't focus on dominating that space?

Poverty is the appropriate answer.

Educate Your Customer: Excite your clients; they should be aware of your entire product offering. Act more innovative and enthusiastic by taking the time to regularly inform your customer of any new additions or changes. View every contact with positivity as both an opportunity to help and as an impetus to increase sales volume. Once they've purchased and established a certain level of trust, how likely are they to try a product you recommend? If they like the product, that will install a certain level of loyalty? The more you keep in touch and serve your customers, the more they are likely to keep coming back and the more likely they are to recommend your services. How would that impact your bottom line?

Reassure Your Clients: How good do you think it would feel as a purchaser to receive a positive press review or a link to an independent website that verifies the reliability and quality of the product you have purchased? How would it affect you as a customer if you were receiving positive updates and recommendations about the products and the company that you do business with? Wouldn't that inspire your confidence to purchase more often? Would it verify your trust in that company?

Probably is the answer.

Because people will gladly buy more products more often from people they like and trust, especially if they have a validated record from others. Pour on those letters of recommendation and testimonials. It's like cream is to coffee. Your job is to continuously let the customer discover they made and are making the right choice by doing business with your firm.

Exclusive Sales: An invitation to an after-hours private sales function for past customers or to an event with promised exceptional value is a real motivator. Inclusive drinks, snacks, local politicians and dignitaries also add that little bit of weight to the event. Plus, promoting it as a network marketing event can add that little bit of spice which brings out additional potential purchasers. Offer a special gift to attendees such as promotional materials if possible.

Joint Incentives: Take on another non-competing company's merchandise, market and sell it for a commission at your event. You should only team up with a reputable company that supplies quality products and applies the same high standards as you do. Make it a win-win situation for all by negotiating and encouraging mutual incentives, because the benefits are rewarding. The other firm should be delighted to have an additional marketing outlet. Consistently check the quality of the other firm's products because assumptions can be costly.

Consistent Vision: At every opportunity drop stickers and flyers on products such as heaters, washing machines, laptops, computers, fridges, cars, radios, pubs and anywhere and everywhere you service. Include a 24 hour number for call out emergencies. Design your message with easy to read fonts and distinctive bright colours. If you were to take a moment and list the benefits of designing your message in this way, what would they be?

Email and Push Marketing Sales: Create demand with past customers on limited edition special offers for past customers only, with inclusion of a purchase deadline. This is easily achieved with phone text push marketing technology. Be sure the customer has downloaded your cure code or agreed to be contacted. Keep the message catchy, short and simple using motivational sales words showing the exact benefit of taking action now! By what percentage do you think you could improve your sales by using this additional technique?

Greeting Cards: In today's modern age, technology seems to have left personal out in the cold. Sending birthday, Christmas, New Year's and cards for all sorts of occasions has become a rarity in connecting with customers. Stand out for success because people love to get cards, especially hand written cards that are not plastered with advertising but are about the occasion. When you take the time to hand write and sign a message it says to the customer that you care because after all isn't that what running a business and creating sales is about? How do you feel when you get a nice card? Ok It is labour intensive and it can be costly, so just send cards to your top clients, the 20% that give you 80% of your turnover. They will love you for it and it helps keep them loyal.

Just a Reminder: This system is particularly good for dentists, doctors, florists and a whole host of repeat service industries. A simple personalized reminder card saying due a service, a check-up, maintenance, cholesterol check etc. is just the ticket, followed by a phone call to confirm will certainly ring up the till on a more regular basis. Information is power and it helps your sales. If you can manage to acquire important dates that relate to your customers personally and use that information in a positive way, what will that do for your relationship with your clients? There are an abundance of contact ideas you can use to show that you care and this is what separates you from the competition. We all need a unique selling proposition (USP) that says this is who my business is and this is why doing business with us is better for you, the customer. If you can manage to collect the special dates of importance belonging to your customers and utilize the file to its fullest potential, then you will turn them into raving fans.

Over Deliver On Your Promise: How do you think the customer feels when you create massive value by over-delivering on your promise? After the product or service has been delivered the customers reflect on your performance and make no mistake about this, they will talk to their colleagues, friends and families about their decision to purchase because they are seeking validation for their actions and that is just human nature. If you have created an exceptional value situation, your client will be proud to announce to the world the wisdom of their decision. They will be only delighted to refer you and they will come back for more. If you have under achieved on your obligation to perform according to the contract, the result will be the death of a line of potential income from several people who know your customer. Your reputation has just died with your inadequate performance. Always have an ace up your sleeve to surprise your customer. Just go that little bit further, go the extra mile and create a raving fan because the related income is exponential.

Consistent Reliability: People admire and respect consistency and reliability. Complacency is a real business killer. Treat your clients like million dollar customers because you have taken so much time and effort to win their loyalty you want to keep them. Your clients start walking when you and your staff are failing to keep your part of the unwritten contract. You've got to be reliable and you've got to be consistent because the longer they do business with you the more they will expect. Remember, your reputation is only as good as the performance you gave the last time you serviced that customer and it is absolutely vital you drum this into your staff. What are the optional decisions you need to make if some of your staff are not on board with the message?

Chapter 9

Raise Your Average Sale Price

Your average sale price is a combination of the accumulated sales divided by the total number of purchases. If you could incrementally improve that situation then why would you not do it? You will find below some ideas on how to accomplish that task. It is vital you take action and get to it. No one idea is better than the next because they all work. Motivate yourself to find the glove that fits for your business and start making more money. Who would benefit from you taking home an additional 10% every month?

Use a Checklist: After you have created some rapport with the customer what would the benefits be to both of you if you were hand them a prepared check list and a pen with the printed associated products they might need for the task at hand ? What would be the effect to the business if every customer got one and you rewarded the sales staff according to their enthusiasm? You may need to tweak the questions on the list as you go along, but remember continuous and never ending improvement creates a thriving business.

Learn To Use Closing Techniques: Questions are the way to raise your average sale price by taking your customer from where they are to where they want to get to. The challenge is that they have resistance in their mind which is of no benefit to them or to you. Masterful use of questions creates miraculous results. You should possess an arsenal of different closes and be proficient in their use, for there is nothing more embarrassing than a sales person attempting sales talk who has never taken the time to upgrade, practice and rehearse their question skills. An earnest attitude to do the necessary preparation will improve your skills and give resounding results. If you could employ just a little innovation to create a more rewarding powerful presentation, then why wouldn't you?

All Payment Systems: Allow cash, cheque, credit card, foreign currency and also include Bit Coin because as soon as you discriminate in any area it usually costs the business money. Be open to receiving all forms of payment that increase your average sale price. You may find that some companies who supply wireless credit card terminals have more favourable terms for you the business owner than others. The benefits of having wireless terminals are, with a mobile device business can be transacted anywhere anytime and it just makes it easier for people to buy.

Consistently Upsell: By upskilling your sales personnel with the correct training on how to sell and having them understand the importance of upselling will maintain their focus. The result will be larger volume, higher transaction rates and improved customer satisfaction. If you take a look at the additional sales figures that are attributed to the phrase would you like a delicious apple pie with that or let me super-size that order for you in McDonalds, it adds to hundreds of millions of dollars annually. The upsell is just the cream on the cake that just might give your business the edge over the competition.

Be Selective: Instead of wasting precious time servicing the 80% of customers that give you 20% of your revenue, work more with the 20% of clients that return 80% of the turnover. Send the timewasters and complainers to your competition. Stick to working and developing improved relationships with grade A and B customers. Treat them all like million dollar customers and remind yourself consistently of the business value they will bring over a lifetime. Reward them for their loyalty, inspire them to introduce referrals and reap the benefit. Happy repeat customers gladly refer if you have built up a strong element of trust in that relationship. Because you already know how important a qualified referral is to your business, when do you think would be the right time to ask your customer the "who do you know" question?

Add Incentives: Refrain from discounting and switch to adding on low margin cost products as an incentive to closing the high margin products. Just refuse to discount your product or service because you come across as lowering your value.

Always Assume the Sale: Demonstrate the highest priced product in that range first and list the benefits that make that item special. If the prospect can't afford the best then they have the opportunity to choose from the rest. If you aim high it gives you the ground to move to a lower priced item. It's a lot easier than going low and trying to march them to the top.

Add Sales Incentives: Keeping score with the daily highest average sales and rewarding staff is a real motivator. Putting targets up in the staff meeting room and openly showing the results helps to create competition and allows all team members to monitor their own progress. Having a team average sales figure with generous rewards encourages the stronger sales persons to help the weaker increase their average. Clear goals and exact targets can help build teamwork, morale, comradery, clarity and certainty.

Posting and Packaging: Always charge for postage and packing because people expect it and nine times out of ten they will just accept it as part of the purchase process. That 5 Euro postage fee might not seem like a lot but when you start getting into shipping thousands of items per year and it's coming out of your bottom line, the five euro per item becomes hugely significant. Always charge more than the actual cost of the postage because the packing is not free and time is the most precious commodity you have. That 1 or 2 euro extra on 10,000 shipped items now sits up and takes notice.

High Margin Products: Stock and sell higher price ranges with higher margins. Focus on premium products and develop a name and image synonymous with quality and better customer service. Dress your staff for success and reward your champions generously. Always have your place of business kept perfectly clean and insure your bathrooms are fit for your mother. Have check lists and monitor your business image rigorously.

Selling Warranty: Extended warranty and add on insurance products are a great addition to your turnover provided the numbers work and there is no labour on your part. Coverage should give the purchaser peace of mind and the added benefit of a no nonsense repair or replacement situation. In the customers mind your value is as good as how you perform your guarantee.

Selling Service Contracts: If you are closing on products that require regular maintenance, then promoting alternate choice in one, three and five year service contracts is the way to go, especially if the warranty coverage is dependent on regular maintenance of their product. It is likely the risk adverse type customer will accept your additional offering, if you can show comparable rates.

Creating Bulk Buy: You don't have to reduce your margin. Just create a bulk buy situation and do not discount. It's far more profitable to add on and it creates a higher revenue stream to simply add on low margin product into the bulk buy mix.

Creative Financing: Collaborate with several lenders and have alternate finance available should your clients require it. Let me point out it should be suitable for them regardless of their past financial situation. There are lenders that may have higher points lending for persons with less than desirable credit. It is helpful as a salesperson to provide solutions for purchasers who have difficulty in assuming credit for the product.

Chapter 10

Increasing Your Margin

There are a variety of different methods to increase your margin. Ultimately if you wish to save and increase your bottom line, you should take the time to discover and implement some or more of the selection of ideas below. There you will find a starting point and it might be prudent to discover additional methods outside this book for further help to achieve that purpose.

Higher Margin Goods: Sometimes the most expensive items do not have the highest margin. Would it be wise to examine your stock or service and push the higher margin items? What would the effect be if you were to discontinue selling low margin items and continuously shift the customer's attention to higher margin products? Know the exact margin on each product or service you sell and make sure your staff knows it too. They should be trained to be aware and understand the importance of the margin.

Price Rise: You've got to raise your prices. The majority of your customers won't even notice and if they do they are unlikely to create a fuss. The perception of fear on a price increase rests with you the business owner. Customers have been trained from birth to expect price rises and the majority do not react to an increase because they have been conditioned to expect it. Get over your fear because FEAR is just false evidence that appears real when it's not. If you do have some customers that complain because of the increase, well you may wish to question the loyalty of those clients because they are probably complainers anyway. Not everyone will be overjoyed with an increase if they even notice. It is possible you may lose some clients but you won't likely lose the good ones. Be brave and focus on the fact that the additional increase will more than compensate for the loss of the complainers. You don't need to highlight the price rise but be prepared to educate your customers if they enquire. Direct their attention to the benefits received, because an educated consumer will usually buy whereas a confused prospect buys nothing. Now that's the way to jump start your margin increase, be brave and be a champion.

Stop Paying Out Overtime: Before you hire the correct staff members and even prior to the presentation of an employment contract make it clear there is no overtime and there never will be. Double time, time and a half and the additional regulatory contributions that go along with it suck the blood from your business like a vampire. Overtime is a huge burden on any business and unless you are feeling like a charity, you need to lose the guilt because there are a lot of other ways you can compensate your star performers. Instead of loading up their tax commitment which drives the employee over the tax threshold and into a higher bracket, one solution could be to allow flexi time which a lot of people love. It empowers the employee in the area of freedom which has a high value on most people's list. It gives freedom to look after their kids, go to college part time and do all sorts of things that people love to do. Offer your employees time off when things are quieter in the week. Allow them to trade off time with each other as long as the business is fully informed and it is approved. You may need to check you have a balanced team for those traded days but make sure you provide the approval or an alternate solution within a short time of the request because it is important for employees to feel empowered.

Stop Unproductive Advertising: If your ads are not generating cash immediately then stop, rethink and re-launch. Advertising only becomes an investment when it's making money. If you keep running the same old ads that are not making more than the cost of the advertising, then your practice is an overhead and a liability. However when you generate an ad that works and it brings in more than it costs it becomes an investment with a positive cash flow. The advertisement then can be an exponential money spinner. Keep doing what works and stop doing what doesn't.

Rent Instead of Owning: Rent is a write off as far as tax is concerned. If you own the building it is an asset and you are also liable for property tax. Perhaps it may be possible to sell the building and lease it back. Discuss it with your accountant or your financial adviser. Surround yourself with expert advice, it worked for Henry Ford.

Choose a Better Accountant: If your accountant is not continuously updating their skills then choose another. Old diplomas on a wall mean nothing - that's out of date news. Look for an accountant who is always updating their skills, the fees could be a bit more expensive but they are likely to save you more than the cost of the additional fee.

Reduce Monthly Overheads: Pay cash rather than having a list of rental agreements. This can be difficult if you don't have a lot of cash available in the early days but find a way as you go along. Buy second hand or try to go without because if you have a couple of sales months with poor results the incurring costs of several different payments can create stress and that's something we want to avoid.

Reduce Your Stock: Excess stock kills cash flow. Spend more time planning what you need ahead of time and be ruthless about it.

Have items delivered as often as necessary and cut down on your driving and shopping time. If you were proactive and calculated how many hours per day, per week, per month and per year would you spend driving?

Slash Costs Over Time: Incremental reductions in all areas over time are cumulative with positive results. Lower your overheads by looking at each systems cost base and get more quotes from more suppliers in each. Contractors, small contractors, freight, post, electricity, gas, office supplies, insurance, maintenance and fees are just a few to be negotiated. Work on it consistently week after week month after month until you've rid the business of the excess tripe. Your aim is to have a lean mean moneymaking machine because that's why you are in business isn't it?

Check Lists, Check Lists: You only get paid to do things once so make sure whatever the task, that it's organized correctly. Remember your employees are as good or as poor as the instruction you provide. The more detail and the more accountability the better their performance will be. If you have a regimented system of check lists that need to be signed and counter signed by a checker you will save yourself a ton of money in time, defective product, waste, consumer relations and unnecessary purchases. If you operate on a 10% margin, things only need go wrong 11% of the time to be in negative profit.

Eliminate Slow Stock: Only stock products that move fast. The more items you have that sit on the shelf the more it costs. Continuously monitor product shelf time because the more items you rotate through the business the greater your cash flow, which is the primary function, correct?

Sack Unmotivated Employees: If they are not working with you, then they are working against you. There is no middle ground; get rid of them and the sooner the better. If you have done everything correctly - that means, provided the right impetus for motivation, communicated clearly, given responsibility, job satisfaction, reward, and the opportunity for good employee/employer relations and things just are just not working, then that person has to go before he or she infects your whole crew. You cannot keep a fester in your ranks.

Negotiate Purchase on Consignment: Only pay when you have sold the product. It frees up your cash for other needs. It's an awesome strategy if you can get it to work.

Bulk buy on hold. Purchase larger orders of fast moving items on agreement of a price freeze over a period of time, with payment only on the monthly consignment deliveries.

Chapter 11

Free Your Mind And The Flow Will Follow

Being active is a key ingredient and you must decide to add to that function day by day. If you were to admit to yourself that you have the opportunity to be an advanced adult in this society and affirm your own bravery by recognizing the steps you are taking, what is that admission likely to do for your confidence?

For every little positive step you take regardless of size, take the time to pat yourself on the back and develop the habit of complimenting yourself, because it's important to build your inner strength.

Try and anticipate situations before they happen. If you were to visualize a situation and see yourself being successful before you take on the task, are you more likely or not to increase the odds of being successful?

Professional Snooker players see the ball going into the pocket many times before they even get down to take the shot and low and behold, something magic happens, 95% of the time the ball goes in. That's not magic, that's just the tool of visualization.

Always be for the positive. You will find there are a lot more people in the positive camp than you realize. It is only when you start to cheer for the positive that like minds will unveil themselves and be attracted to you. Be and feel alive in everything you do. Through your own will, you can choose to feel alive and vibrant or you can choose to be dead because there is no one going to help you with that one unless you pay them a substantial hourly fee. These are just some of the additional decisions you need to make for yourself.

Keep up with technology and fashion, because the more you keep up with technology, the more confident you will feel knowing you have additional tools in your kit bag. When I say keep up, that means be aware, but spend your time on the A rated tasks that are going to make you money. There's no point in spending 4 hours a day playing with the latest gadget if it's not helping you turn your economy around. Keep up with fashion because the better you dress the better you feel, but keep it business attire for business. During the day, Monday to Friday always be dressed and ready to do business.

Refuse to argue and avoid rising to the bait of confrontation. Decline to put yourself in the situation where you argue with a prospect or client for several reasons. First off it's disrespectful. If you come off as a bag of emotions you'll lose the sale, lose the client and probably a valuable account which could result in you losing your job and losing your economy that you worked so hard to build. With arguing it's all lose. Allow calmness to prevail so you can think and outmanoeuvre your opponent. Allow the other person to lose the head. Keep eye contact and use a neutralizing phrase such as! *"I can understand why you might feel that way"*. Be genuine and respond with *"I understand where you are coming from"*, *"yes I understand"*, *"yes I understand"* until the other person blows themselves out and then you will gain control of the situation. Nine times out of ten they will begin to apologize and then you come back with" I understand where you are coming from". At this point you have controlled the situation and the prospect or client will be more willing to hear your proposal. You must be flexible like the willow bending and flowing in the breeze, which allows you to return to your original position. That's how a professional handles the situation as opposed to being an amateur who gets into a heated argument. People become amused by your poise in tough negotiating situations and you become the angel of the office. You get noticed. Search for others on a similar growth path and become as human as possible.

Satisfy your mind by asking questions of yourself synonymous with growth and spirituality. Exact the growth and intelligence that is your right. Agree to set yourself free and arrive at your desired destination. Seek out the knowledge of the natural laws of the universe and awaken yourself from the cellar of winter into the delicious light of spring. Move forward into the foreground of fortune and good luck. Awaken the beauty within and start a new beginning. You have a choice and you have free will and you can choose to be ahead of the crowd from which the best of life will flow. Stay sharp in your mind and white in your soul, by being interested in amusing and exciting beneficial projects.

Become so excited that you catch the centre of probability, which leads to certainty. Constant clear plans that allow for changeability are far more economic in distance and effort and bring success faster than rigid directions without change that take you off route.
Open your mind to clever and ingenious input from wherever you can find it. Let the sunshine flow from a life of comedy rather than serious drama. Leave drama and tragedy alone. Don't even give it your attention. Free yourself from the negativity of newspapers, news and other peoples' dramas. Keep the thoughts in your head simple and sunshine like. Genuinely compliment people you see here and about and your day will blossom. Refrain from comment regardless of who the person is or wherever they might be. Volunteer if you can. You will be astounded, not only with the satisfaction you receive from your efforts but with the connections you will meet through your efforts.

Continue to be constant in the construction of your courageous new self. Remember to continuously compliment yourself for even the smallest of the steps you take. Always have the courage to do what is correct because not being honest can destroy all that you have endeavoured to create.

Those who champion humanity and kindness laugh through life in security and safety and ride on to success. When you awaken, decide to think in the light, make that conscious choice so that you fully feel the birth of a new day and appreciate that you are alive. Attack your daily challenges with passion and carry yourself on to victory. Be consciously aware of your arrival at each new destination as your vision becomes reality. Visualize, feel, believe and you will bring forth your reality. Build and construct your own republic within yourself. Deflect other's failed negative dictatorships. Live your life and treat others as you would like to be treated, for it is easy to look at others as though they are different and it's easy to be distant because prejudice is a difficult disease to overcome. Clean your mind and treasure its health. Divorce it from being dirty or influenced by vice. Create and unite your body, mind and soul into one harmony.

Get to the upstairs of your mind. Don't worry about emigration because you don't need a green card to go there. You can come up with a billion dollar idea in the shower one morning, get on a plane, arrive in another country and you don't have to pay any import duty. You don't even have to declare it. Some people never declare their ideas and they never make any money. They stay poor. If you have a news flash in your head with a great idea, act on it, write it out, tease it out will all positivity. It is the Universe giving you the go fuel. Don't wait, act on it. The universe is saying it's time to do something. Move on, live life and prosper. Whatever your beliefs you should still do something. Fine tune your intuition and listen to it.

Friends are so nice to enjoy. It feels ever so nice when we meet friends. We enjoy pets because they bring out a feeling that feels good. Feeling good is about the most important thing you can do in business and your life. Feeling good is on the opposite polarity of feeling bad and you have a choice, to feel good or to feel bad. It's as simple as that. Feeling bad, depressed, upset insulted, hurt or whatever negative mode you fancy is a choice. You can, by force of will, turn not only the moment, the day, week, month or your life around, by focusing on things that make you feel good when you think of them. The simple trick is to spend more time thinking and feeling about things that make you feel good than things that make you feel bad. When you can spend most of your day doing that you've taken a giant leap in mastering your life!

Death, disease, divorce, division, drama and a whole host of other dirty little dastardly lies are what come directly from you, in the way you think and the way you talk. Why not choose health, cleanliness, unity, life, laughter and fun. It's your choice. Expand your horizons in positive, interesting, domestic and foreign matters. Make space for comedy and fun. Make space for things that make you feel good. If you like to meditate and that makes you feel good, then do that. If you want to eat a salami sandwich and that makes you feel good then do that. Concentrate on doing whatever makes you feel good and live day by day in that flow.

Success asks you include and examine everything different. Your mind thrives on variety. Seek exciting positive material. Feed your brain until it becomes a ravenous animal for the truth, because a sheltered mind is a cheap import?

Success and failure are choices. They are at opposite ends of a pole. It's a very simple proposition! You can be one of the few who are correct and true or you can be one of the many who are not. Courage will conquer fear and find success as increased success is drawn to increased courage; this is a basic universal law.

Before you begin a task, visualize the finish in your mind. Just as a professional soccer player sees the pass before he kicks the ball, see the result before you take action. Refrain from walking on hilly ground and upper limiting. By this I mean self-sabotaging your efforts. Take the easiest, most direct route on flat ground. Do not believe your endeavour should be a struggle or it will be. Why should it be? Because your parents and colleagues and everyone you've ever listened to said life should be a struggle.

You've been programmed to think in ways for various reasons which were not in your interest.

Life is meant to be abundant and full of joy. If that's where you focus your mind, if that's what you decide it to be and that's what you believe it to be then that's how it will be. Of course you can decide to have it all dark and full of pain, but that's up to you.

Forbid thy self to follow the crowd, and allow yourself forward into the foreground of fortune. Be brave and take the lead for yourself. Whether you are a native or a foreigner in whichever country you live, let not yourself be arrested by domestic or foreign economies. Melt the freeze that has held your past. Free your present of the stale and move into a full and wonderful future.

Find out what it is that you are best at. What is it you really love to do? You might ask, well how do I find out if that's the right thing for me or not? The answer is within, if you love doing something and you can spend hour after hour doing it without feeling as if it's work, then that's a clue. If you love doing what you are doing, then you are more than likely going to be a success and more successful than the next man because you really love your occupation, whereas he may be doing it because he was told that it was a good profession and guided to it by well-meaning family member or a school guidance counsellor. Does this ring a bell? Then listen to the bell and make a change.

Chapter 12

Questions You Should Be Asking Yourself

No problem ever thought up by man, could not be solved by man. If you can come up with the challenge, you can come up with the solution.
RDB

What are you willing to do to achieve your goal?

Here are a few questions you may find it wise to answer with pen and paper in your success journal or personal diary. These questions are designed to get you to think about your position and improve your personal power. Answer them in the positive.

How motivated are you and where do you get your inspiration from? Because the more reasons you have the more motivated you will be.

Do you think it would be wise to get those reasons down on paper and continuously find more?

Are you willing to work long and hard to master your business?

What are the key motivating factors for you?

Is it providing for your children's' education?

Is it success?

What is the number one reason you decided to start this endeavour?

Is it the feelings that you get from the reasons you focus on, is that why you do it?

Then seek out more feelings that you want and you will find more motivation.

What is unique about your business?

Why should people want to spend money on your product or service?

Are you spelling out in a clear and concise manner what makes your business or service that little bit different so that people understand what you are offering them?

Is it possible you could improve the message?

Why do customers need what you are selling?

Who needs it?

Because we know, most people don't care about you or your product. How can you get them to care about what you are offering?

Can you deliver your proposition in 60 seconds so it compels someone to listen?

What do potential customers crave?

Ask yourself what steps can I take to deliver more benefit to my customers than the competition?

How can I create an advantage over my competitors?

Which benefits can I add that my competitors don't?

Lower price, better design and instant gratification are some benefits customers love. Are there any additional benefits you can come up with?

Is it easier and more profitable to own a larger piece of a smaller market with less competition? Or owning a tiny piece of a huge market with massive competition?

How can I define and dominate my market?

If you tend to serve just a few large customers, is it likely they will have more power to negotiate discounts? It's something you need to be aware of and keep an eye on.

If you use just one supplier you will be at the mercy of that business eventually. Source your product materials from different suppliers.

If you can see the profitability of your business, there are many others just like you. Investigate how easy it would be for a new business to steal your customers because there is always a cheaper, faster, newer way to deliver a product or service.

How important is it to defend your company by being ahead of the potential new competition?

There will always be setbacks and learning curves; the secret is to learn from other people's mistakes.

If you could model an already successful operation to cut potential mistakes, frustration, time and loss of revenue from your endeavour, how would that sit with you?

If risk makes you throw up, get over it. Get a napkin, clean up and get on with the tasks at hand because you'll never score a goal from the bench.

Condense time and make it your best friend. Know what time is doing every minute of the day, because your time is finite and you can't make any more of it. What would happen to your earnings if you were to do the most important thing at every given moment?

Funding your own operation is expensive but you only answer to yourself. While using other people's money can be cheaper, sometimes it gets messy and you become accountable. Which values are most important to you in sequence?

If you could outsource your sales function to distributers and smaller resellers would you? Sales people are motivated by the measure of their success - money. They look after their own interests first and are driven indirectly to surge your bottom line. Hire someone who is already successful and let the juniors mirror their model.

Do not recruit from friends. Get in the right people because having the right ingredients helps the dough rise. Using outside advisors you respect, who are not afraid to give their opinion can be a great benefit.

For increased revenue and motivation tie employee bonus pay to customer satisfaction forms. How do you think that will affect the business?

Chapter 13

The Structure of a Sale

There is no magic bullet in sales but there is every possibility you can increase your earnings if you take a serious look at what happens on the sales stage. This next chapter is a breakdown of the sales process as I understand it and how it works for me. I use variations of qualification questions and different closes in all types of conversations depending on the situation. Your aim should be to fully understand the process and equip yourself to be competent in whatever sales arena you find yourself. Over time you will develop your own unique style. The more you close, the faster you will develop your own closing habits. If you can grasp a combination of the points I make in this chapter and use them in a structured sequence with relevant question and closing techniques, you will see a significant increase in your bank balance.

A Confused buyer buys nothing, whereas when you educate a qualified prospect you get paid.

RDB

Bonding: Key issue here, people will only buy from those that they like and trust, unless you are the only supplier in town. So you better work hard on your interpersonal skills and learn to ask open ended questions. You need genuine sincerity and you need to learn to listen. Most people are not as interested in listening to what you have to say as what they have to say themselves. Enjoy the ride, gather the information and allow the other person to become more comfortable by letting them talk. You should be using pre-qualification questions at the outset, and lots of them. The more time you spend prequalifying your prospects, the more you will close and the more money you will make with the least amount of effort. By asking bonding type questions and allowing the other person to expand, they relax a little and that's the direction we want to head.

Guarantee: You must have it. If you want to disarm your prospects and put them in a safe frame of mind then push it. Your guarantee should be printed in bold for all to see. It should be on your business cards, literature, proposals, agreements, contracts, even your office wall and everywhere your client turns their head because the more they see the guarantee, the more relaxed they'll be. You have to say it with a question also, for example: "Mr. Prospect, how important is it for you to have a no nonsense money back guarantee when a person invests in a product or service?" (P) "Absolutely essential." (You)" On a scale of 1 – 10 how important do you think that is?" (P) "Well it's a 10." (you) "That's exactly the way I feel myself and that's why we have it."

Promise: Your promise should be directly linked to the guarantee and related to the performance, reliability and soundness of the product or service for a specific period of time. You need to be careful here. There are very few products or services for which you can provide a lifetime warranty for. Never promise on something you cannot deliver. The promise is a "precursor" for the guarantee within a specific time period designed, to show confidence in your product / service and gain the prospects trust. The golden rule is, if you make a promise then always deliver or your reputation will suffer. The promise should be written in the same vicinity and delivered at the same time as your guarantee.

Preamble: A preamble is exactly what it sounds like. You explain to the prospect how you are going to make the presentation before you make the presentation. It promotes clarity by giving the prospect a good idea of what is going to happen while at the same time you are continuously building rapport.

The Owner/Contractor Relationship: Using discovery questions about past experiences and what's most important in a future relationship helps builds trust and permission to proceed. It is very important to understand the nature of the relationship your future client is willing to accept.

Target Performance: Uncovering the targets where your prospect sees his company's position in the short, medium and long term helps you understand more clearly how you can be of assistance.

End Users: Understanding who these employees are and where their mind set may be, and being aware of how your proposal affects them is important because there is always some resistance to a new proposal, product or idea. You want the end user to get on board because it's possible you might need that extra advocate to get the sale over the line. Discover what is likely to be important to the end user and use it to your advantage in the form of questions.

Ownership: Whoever it is that takes ownership and responsibility for the proposal, product or service within the company is a key player who you may need to connect with because that person is likely, in most cases, to have an impact on the buying decision. This person needs to be handled delicately and given the recognition for the position they hold.

Urgency: Without urgency there is no need for the product and no need for you to be in that meeting. Without urgency your proposal is a complete waste of time. So there better be a genuine need or you better be able to uncover an unforeseen need through discovery type questions that highlights the imminent lack. Never waste your time giving a presentation to an unqualified prospect because there is no need and it is a waste of your most precious commodity.

Financial Status: Through a series of qualification questions you should be able to understand the financial impact of the proposal and have the ability to gauge fairly quickly the positive and negative impact of your proposal. If it's not going to have a positive impact for the other party, then you need to step back. If the financial weight of the proposal outweighs the take-off/ benefits, then it stays at the terminal for now or until there is something lighter.

Financial Consideration: How is this proposal, service or product going to be paid for? What methods should be considered? Highlight the return on investment through discovery type questions. Open ended questions that allow the prospect come up with the answers are genius because if I say it, then it's open to question but if the prospects says it then it's absolutely true.

Bank Arrangement: Be smart enough to have a network of competitive friendly lenders who make it possible for your prospects to acquire the offering through a hassle free financial arrangement. The benefits are myriad because you have assumed the role of a solution provider in the eyes of the prospect, which inspires their confidence in you. This leads to a greater chance of closing the sale and the prospect doesn't need to jump through hoops to own the product.

Past Performance: It is advantageous to introduce your past clients to your new client through a serious of well worded testimonials because if you say how good you are it's open to question but when others are raving fans and announce it to the world, your credibility goes up in the eyes of the prospect. Always remember, what we are engaged in, is the education of prospects which nullifies resistance.

Technical Ability: Through a serious of earlier searching questions that uncovered the need, you should be able to highlight the benefits of your offering. To highlight the technical ability of your product or service, educate the prospect with a subtle relayed series of closing questions, using alternate choice. For example, " the unit can perform X and Y or would you prefer it to create C and D. "C and D please. "Ok you need C and D, let me make a note of that, and so on. You then continue to close with pre-learned structured closing questions which you should know by heart.

Relevant Experience: Through earlier qualification questions you discovered what was important to the prospect. Now is the time to use that information by bringing it to the forefront. Remind the prospect of the earlier statement and get him to confirm what he said. Then highlight the benefit of your own company's experience and the solution you provide in a close.

Quality, Standards and Guarantee: You have already agreed to put your guarantee on your stationery, business-cards, proposal forms and contracts. What you do next is simple - discuss it with the client. Bring it up in the form of a question like: *"Mr prospect, how important is it for you to have a no nonsense money back time limited guarantee, if the product or offering does not do what I'm telling you it's going to do?"* If he accepts the guarantee, he's just bought it.

Maintenance Costs: Discuss it with the prospect, ask a related question and bring the objection out in the open before the prospect does. Uncover his fears, and then cover that base with a solution, a highlighted benefit, followed with a tie down.

Cost Overruns: Again, you bring it up, bring it out, pat it on the head and then you put it to bed.

Schedule Overruns: Handle it like any of the other objections. You announce it, give it the required significance, gauge the importance, validate the fear, provide the solution, highlight the benefit of the solution and let the prospect affirm the significance of the solution by asking the right type of question.

Completed Projects: Opportunity time - WATCH THIS SPACE. When you create an agreement on the importance and benefits of your company analysing the completed projects over time, and the effect of your offering, you create several potential opportunities. 1 You've moved the prospect much closer to authorization. 2 You have created confidence in your after sales service. 3 You have created a long term contract. 4 you have created possibilities for add-on products over time and 5 you have put yourself in primary position for a renewal and you can seriously look at the lifetime potential earnings from this customer.

Now Let's Get Down to the Bread and Butter.

Up to this point we have been qualifying and bringing out potential objections before the client does. Through the skilful art of using expanding probing questions we provide the prospect with solutions. We then highlight the benefit of the solution by allowing the prospect to affirm that benefit as an answer to yet another question. It's all part of an ongoing structure that requires a continuous flow of positive responses from the prospect. In fact we are moving the prospect into a habit of saying yes because it just makes sense to do so.

We now continue on this path and the end line is within sight. Now we want to get paid, but before we get paid we've got to explain our level of commitment, how much we care and what is involved in our effort to serve the client.

Prospects don't care until you show them how much you care.

NB: As you go through these last sections of the close, you have a proposal sheet with the prospect details filled in as much as possible. You will have a little check box at the side of each paragraph and a couple of blank lines under each section. The reason for this is to get a yes by saying to the prospect; "do you understand how that works?" or "do you understand that?" or "are you ok with that?" These are all little test closes because it is an accumulation of test closes that lead to the final close. The couple of lines down below are for the alternate close. Would you like that in mint green or screaming pink? Whatever the answer, you say, let me make a note of that. Every time you check the box and make a note of what you have discovered about the prospect's needs through a question, write it down and move on.

Management Capability: "If you remember our earlier conversation Mr Prospect, how important you said it was to have confidence in dealing with management that is capable of delivering the type of service or product that you want." I get him to reaffirm the recognition of the fact with a yes as an answer to a question. I then move on to the next yes acquisition.

Past Performance and Quality: I'm gently just moving into another confidence builder here. I am again reminding you about how important you said it is to you, and also through a well-placed question I am covertly directing you to bring up references and testimonials that confirm the positive recommendation of my firm that you are seeking.

Project Management Organization: How we do what we do and how that benefits you and your company. Why it is important for you and affirmed again in a series of yes or positive responses builds more credibility and moves us towards authorization.

Program of Works: As I walk you through the blue print that explains what is involved in the creation of the offering and get you to acknowledge the effort you begin to confirm our worth.

Associated Time per Project: Explain what's involved, followed up by benefits; recognition and having the prospect highlight the benefit because he sells himself. Simply check the box and say "let me make a note of that."

Design: This is all about bringing out the dream with alternate choice type and expansive questions. If your product involves producing a design, then you must get a design fee because design is not free and neither is your time. I remind you once again because of its importance that time is the most precious commodity you have. You can keep on making money, but you can't make time, once it's gone it's gone. 2 When you get a design fee it confirms the prospect is going ahead. 3 At least if they back out, which is highly unlikely after they've paid the fee, you have been paid for your time. So be really tough on that one.

Materials: It is important for the prospect to understand what is involved in the construction of the proposal and you can use that educating process as a continuous sequence of closes such as colour, surface, texture, base etc. The end result is all about the incremental flow of gentle closing. Ticking the box, "do you understand?" "Yes I understand that "then make a note of the alternate choice in the two spaced lines. Do this with every section.

Labour: It is my belief the prospect should have a grip on the intensity of labour in a product at times because it allows them to justify paying for the offering in their own head. You see when you guide them to come up with their own conclusions in your favour, it is their idea and it's not open to question. It allows the prospects to feel and justify the price because they think they are getting value for money. Again, tick the box "let me make a note of that."

Delivery: there are a host of different opportunities for you to close using the delivery as a base for alternate choice. Learn numerous closes off by heart because once they have chosen, they have effectively bought the product. Again, tick the box "let me make a note of that."

Installation: How, when, and where the prospect wants the product installed or delivered is a closers dream world. It opens a variety of different situations to zero in on, finalizing the sale? "Mrs. Doyle if you already had that cabinet now, knowing that the room is ready for it, where would you put it? " "Let me make a note of that" "Assuming Mr O Reilly that you are happy with the design and it does everything you want, can you see us installing it in the morning or do you think it would be better to do it late in the afternoon after the staff have left?" "Let me make a note of that"

Variations: There are exponential opportunities to use different methods of closing but you need to take the time to study and learn by heart at least a hundred different closes or variations because the more closes you learn to deliver effectively the higher your earnings will go as you transcend from incompetence to competence. Always remember this: "you are as professional as the money you make". After each close you gently smile and say "thank you, let me make a note of that"

Total Investment: Never use terms like, price or cost, they just create negative connotations in the prospect's mind. Phrases such as the monthly amount, the monthly investment, the total investment are much more agreeable.

Deposit: To receive a deposit is vital in any business for several reasons, because it confirms the commitment on behalf of the purchaser. It effectively ties them into the commitment to proceed.

Cash flow is the biggest issue for small businesses by far and collecting a large percentage deposit at the outset, or after the design has been delivered eliminates the cash flow problem. One of the most serious hurdles I come across is business people not having the confidence to ask for the deposit and the will walk away if the other party is not willing to come up with the deposit.

If you have done everything properly, prequalified the prospect over and over and over as you continued to close, shown validated testimonials, explained what was involved in the offering and gained continuous agreement and made all the relevant notes on the already partially filled proposal, then there will be no issue about a deposit because you have built a level of trust and rapport that is acceptable to your prospect. You must ask for the money because you need to gain freedom as you release that cash flow yolk from around your neck.

Design fee: This is a close: "Mrs Doyle let me step back for a moment, "as we agreed", get her to nod, then you begin to go back over all the things you and Mrs Doyle agreed on and I explained this and that and so on and so on and delivery will be on such a date and the total in your total investment, or your final amount except the design fee of x amount which I will take in cash , cheque or credit card , you smile and say" if you would ok the paperwork I will gladly get started on it Tuesday". Gently swing round the proposal documentation towards the prospect hand her a pen and shut up.

Note the design fee should be equal to the value of time you have taken to prepare this proposal plus the value of the time it will take to design the product.

Never say to a prospect, "please sign the contract". Use better words like: "If you wouldn't mind please ok the paperwork and I'll get started" or "if you would authorize the form I will prepare your new blank, "or something of that nature. It's just a more gentle approach.

Chapter 14

Typical Reasons Why Sales People Fail to Close

The majority of sales people feel and believe putting pressure on a prospect is a bad thing. They have been taught that it is not right to put pressure on a prospect. They have been programmed with the idea that it is rude and inappropriate. That's just one of the reasons 20% of the closers in every industry make 80% of the money. You have been taught to accept "no" from your youth and that my friend, is a serious detriment to your income if you are a salesperson. You need to push through to demonstrate you are sold on your product.

A lot of sales people find it uncomfortable to deal with the emotional discomfort though the sales process and getting from no to yes. Regardless of how emotional the prospect gets, stay calm and close the deal. That person may have had a previous frustrating experience you failed to uncover in the pre-qualification process. Learn to sit quietly as your client goes off emotionally, lose the battle, and win the war and the sale.

A Lack of Belief in Your Product or Service: You have to believe that your product is better for this person at a deeper level than the combination of objections they can raise. He who is sold and most convinced will do the most selling. You either do the closing or you will be closed. Which option do you prefer and which option will give you most money?

An incorrect estimation of effort to close the sale will cost you lots of money over and over and over again. A lack of preparation in detail, planning, training, rehearsal, visualization and lack of staying power will prevent you and your family getting paid. What would your life be like and by how much would your bank account be positively affected if you managed to do the most important things to get paid? You wouldn't steal from someone else's pocket would you? Then why would you steal from yourself and your children by not preparing properly? Train for the most difficult customers and hope for the easier ones. If you train properly and use the correct mental attitude, money will rain upon you.

Urgency to Complete: If it's not closed it's a no sale. It's nothing. Sales people with unclosed sales are punished without mercy. Because you did not properly qualify the prospect and you have used up your most valuable resource, time. The market will adjust your thinking by the rewards it does not give you. If you understand there is no purchase without urgency, when would be a good time to start focussing on urgency?

Having no financial plan and no personal financial plan will hold you back. Being consistently aware and focusing on your own financial situation will create urgency and cause you to become a great closer because you are focused. If your financial purpose is high, so will be your earnings. 95% of people do not have a financial plan. That's why the 5% make it. Which group do you insist on belonging to, because there is no middle ground?

Incorrectly Handling Objections: Put in the time to learn, practice and rehearse how to handle objections and stalls. The alternative is poverty over a comfortable lifestyle. You cannot afford not to spend the time learning because it will cost you much more time and lots of money. Most objections are just complaints. Treat all objections as complaints until you hear differently.
A lack of closing material and closing materials and techniques, prevents the close. Great closers have a deep reservoir of material that allows the buyer to make a correct decision for themselves.

You, as the closer, can be the biggest obstacle to the sale. Learn to shut up and listen to the flow of questions you should be asking. You should be asking an abundant series of closing questions and listening more than talking. Let the prospect bring themselves to the sale by answering questions. Your function is just to ask guiding questions.

Unbelievable is a great word because it just about covers everything. The next time someone asks you, how is business and it's not going so well you can say UNBELIEVABLE but make sure you say it with a passionate tone. You won't be lying but you will be covering the ground you want to cover.

Chapter 15

Sales Rules 101

There are a basic set of rules for doing business. If you stick to the principles you will get along just fine. Sometimes you may need to adjust for a particular situation but on the whole the principles in his book are fundamentally sound.

Always ensure both parties are seated when negotiating because you improve the odds of selling dramatically when the prospect is seated. If your prospect stands up in the middle of the negotiation, don't move, just stay seated and it's more than likely the prospect will sit back down. Your calm asserts authority and creates control.

Present your proposal in writing because that which is written is more valued than that which is heard. Always have a legal pad and write down every valued point of discussion. You may have a great memory but what level of embarrassment are you prepared for and what does it cost when you make an error?

Lack of clarity creates confusion, plus, a confused buyer buys nothing. Rehearse your questions to communicate the offer, including the benefits clearly. No one will trust a person who does not speak with clarity. People purchase in normal situations when a level of trust has been established.

Maintain eye contact because it is vital for building trust during the negotiation process. How do you feel when a salesperson refuses to maintain eye contact? Are you more likely to do business or not with a person who shifts their eyes away from you? Would it raise an eye brow for you?

Always have 2 pens with you, because the only way you can close is with a pen. A nice pen can be used as a guidance tool as you walk the prospect through the sales document where you tick the boxes and make a note of the alternate choice closes. If you were to use the tools I'm giving you in this book what is the likelihood you will close more sales?

Try to use humour to relieve uncomfortable silence in the early minutes of the meeting. In some situations humour may not be appropriate but in general humour that makes your client feel good is a benefit of building rapport. So what are the benefits of building rapport?

Always Ask One More Time: After you have had a rejection, continue to ask. Figure out how to re-group and return with another request through a different angle. Ask again and again and again until they say yes. Try to route back until you get the answer you are looking for. Winners never quit. When a child continuously asks for a product while shopping at the store with Mom, is there a likely chance they will get what they want with continued persistence?

The answer is probably.

Always Have an Arsenal of Closes Available so You Don't Repeat Yourself: The average sales person knows very few closes and that's why most are poor. If you did concentrate on closing techniques and learned forty to fifty different types of closes that moved you from the eighty per cent group that shared twenty per cent of the money to the twenty per cent group that share eighty per cent of the money earned, then why wouldn't you?

Always Stay with the Buyer and Maintain Credibility: Leaving the room establishes lack of credibility. You cannot close if you are not there. Bouncing in and out of the presentation will get you a big fat no every time, how stupid and avoidable is that? Properly prepared sales professionals have all the tools and documentation available prior to the appointment. If you need an adjustment on terms during the negotiation try and have your sales manager pre twigged to come to the conference room.

Assume the Sale: You will increase your closing ratio by 33% if you take the time to mentally prepare and visualize the sale from start to close. If you don't know how to visualize I suggest you make it a priority. All top earners know and practice visualization before they meet the prospect, that's another reason they are top producers. Your income solely depends on your mind being in the correct money making state.

Know you Will Come to an Agreement: Keep on saying to yourself during the sales presentation they will do some business and they most likely will.

A maintained positive demeanour is critical regardless of any surprises. When someone drops a clanger on you, how you handle that moment can make or break the business relationship. If you were to use the phrase" that's interesting" what effect would it have on the conversation?

Smile: Regardless of the situation throughout the closing sequence keep smiling. As you tick each box, just smile gently and say "let me make a note of that" then come back with another alternate choice close and repeat the exercise again and again.

Always treat prospects like they will do business. If you treat them in a certain manner they will tend to act in that manner,

When you receive a low ball offer, be grateful for the communication because when someone makes even a low offer they are moving in the right direction. So acknowledge the offer and then move back into your closes.

Always agree with the buyer because as far as the buyer is concerned, what he just said is the absolute truth. Whatever you say is open to question. To resolve the conflict just agree by saying "I hear you," "I understand where you're coming from" and the disagreement is over. What are the benefits of dissolving the conflict instead of keeping it going?

Look for solutions because there are usually loads of alternatives the more you think about the challenge. You can be in the 99% of losers with no answers or you can relish being part of the 1% group of go to guys with the can do attitude. Always find a way to close the deal. If you are committed you will be creative. Continuously ask "what can we do here to make this work?" Ask the prospect "What can you do here to help me make this work for both of us?"

Care so much that you refuse to not close. Make it your mission to help that prospect get the product that they want, need or desire. You know they want, need or desire the goods or service from your prequalification process. So help them gain, by helping them lose whatever is standing in their way. How come charity workers are so effective at their vocation? Could it be their purpose and passion knows no bounds?

Get well versed in an abundance of closes. Again and again I cannot over emphasize this point. The more you learn the more you will earn. Drill, practice and rehearse closes. How much money do you want to earn per day, per week, per month? It is all directly related to the quality of questions you ask yourself and the quality of the questions you ask in your closing sequences. It's a clear choice, and again I'm asking you, how much money do you want to earn?

Know this: you do not provide a service until you close. Until you get the cheque, the cash, credit card details or the agreed compensation, you do not have a contract of sale. You have nothing, just words. You are only as professional as the money you make, not the potential money you make. The money is the measure of how professional you are and what you are worth. Save yourself from stress, heartache, poverty and disappointment by learning to close and accept nothing is anything until you are paid.

Remember, you are not here to do the hard sell, those days are long passed. You are here to satisfy people's wants by helping them get from where they are now to where they want to be through educating and letting them make their own decisions so they overcome their fears and obstacles through the use of ownership questions.

There are an infinite amount of closes that suit an infinite amount businesses and business situations. What I have done here is endeavoured to give you a taste of the real world and the uplifting possibilities of changing your own destination by changing your own economy. You are only limited by the limitations you place within your own mind. When man focussed on running and breaking the four minute mile record, he got just that. When man focussed on going to the moon he got just that too. When Thomas Edison focused on making a light bulb, he made it, even after ten thousand experiments he did not give up, and he got what he focussed on. You too will get exactly what you focus your mind on, whether it is good or bad. It depends on where you put your focus, and if that is changing your own economy and making money, then that is exactly what you will get.

There is only one thing in this universe that you as a human being have been given complete control over and that is the most powerful and special gift given by the creator.

That gift is the ability for you to take control of, and direct your own mind to whatever purpose you wish to achieve. It is a fabulously wealthy gift that knows no natural boundaries. Use it wisely and enjoy the benefits it can produce for its produce is only limited by your beliefs.

Until the next time,
Roger David Barry